Baby Animals

A very first picture book

Nicola Tuxworth

LORENZ BOOKS

Chicks

Let me out, I'm squashed!

I'm a baby chicken.

Hello, Mum!

Rabbits

I'm a baby rabbit. I love crisp lettuce…

…and crunchy carrots.

Time for
a wash ...

...and
a great big
cuddle.

Piglets

I'm a baby pig.

My nose is called a snout.

Did
someone
say dinner?

Mmm,
it smells
good!

Kittens

I'm a baby cat.

Keep still!

Whoops, have I made a mess?

Foals

I'm a
baby
horse.

Look at
my long,
thin legs!

Let's play, Mum!

Ducklings

How do you do?

We're baby ducks.

Let's go
for a
swim.

Can I
come
too?

Puppies

I'm a baby dog.

Oh good, it's time for a walk!

I'm tired now...

...let's have a little nap with bear.

Kids

We're baby goats.

Where
has our
friend
gone?

Here
I am!

We're all
baby animals.
Do you know
our names?

rabbit

chick

puppy

kitten

duckling

This edition published in 1997 by Lorenz Books

© 1997 Anness Publishing Limited

Lorenz Books is an imprint of
Anness Publishing Limited,
Hermes House,
88-89 Blackfriars Road,
London SE1 8HA

This edition distributed in
Canada by Raincoast Books,
8680 Cambie Street, Vancouver,
British Columbia V6P 6M9

ISBN 1 85967 516 6

A CIP catalogue record for this book
is available from the British Library.

Publisher: Joanna Lorenz
Managing Editor, Children's Books:
    Sue Grabham
Editor: Roz Fishel
Special Photography: Lucy Tizard
Stylist: Marion Elliot
Design and Typesetting:
    Michael Leaman Design Partnership

Thanks to Chilli Bernstein, Milo Clare and
Chanelle Robinson for modelling for this book.
Many thanks also to Pampered Pets, Holloway Road,
London.Picture credits: Warren Photographic/Jane Burton -
p5, p12, p13, p14, p15; Zefa - p4 (top), p8, p9, p18, p19.

Printed in Hong Kong / China
10 9 8 7 6 5 4 3 2